THE ELECTRIC RAILWAY THAT NEVER WAS

York—Newcastle 1919

by
R.A.S. HENNESSEY

ORIEL PRESS LIMITED

ISBN 0 85362 087 3

Published by
ORIEL PRESS LIMITED
32 Ridley Place, Newcastle upon Tyne NE1 8LH, England

Printed by Tyne Printing Works, Newcastle upon Tyne

The Background

It is often and rightly said that Tyneside, the land of George and Robert Stephenson, of William Hedley and the waggonways, is the 'cradle of the railways'. Before the Great War it was the home of shipbuilding, heavy engineering and coal mining; it was also becoming a major centre of electrical engineering and was associated with many leading names in the electrical world: the Hon. Charles Parsons, Charles Merz and Sir Joseph Wilson Swan.

By natural affinity the North East merged two of its industries and pioneered electric railways in Great Britain: a 28-mile suburban system from Newcastle to the coast, and further south, in County Durham, a 15-mile mineral line. It was only by the slightest margin that the North East failed to make the hat-trick and electrify a main line before any other British railway. It nearly happened, and if it had the cradle of railways would have seen the birth of the 'new railway' — the high-speed intercity type of line which is now, rather late in the day, all the rage.

The idea of electrifying the York-Newcastle main line of the then North Eastern Railway (NER) came very close to realization in 1919-1922. A magnificent electric express locomotive was built at Darlington, tests and feasibility plans appeared, negotiations were in hand. But the plan, launched confidently amidst stimulating post-war optimism, fizzled out with the ephemeral Lloyd George era. The reality of the 1920's (especially in the North East) was much grimmer: staple industries declined and unemployment mounted; the *Economist* called 1921, with its 6% unemployment rate, 'one of the worst years of depression since the industrial revolution' — hardly the best background for a million-pound electrification.

Before 1914, however, in the North East's golden age, the regional economy prospered. It led the country in the adoption of new techniques; for instance in the application of electric power to industry. Although its first electric power companies dated from 1889[1] it is more relevant here to note the building of Neptune Bank Power Station at Wallsend in 1901 by the Walker & Wallsend Union Gas Company, who were diversifying their interests. The station was master-minded by Charles Merz, the 'young meteor' of electricity, who was to become the leading consultant of his day, and co-founder of the famous consulting engineers Merz & McLellan (M & M). Neptune Bank was the first station to supply the now standard 3-phase a.c. for industrial purposes, albeit at the now odd values of 5kV, 40 cps.

Merz pressed the case of electrification at all relevant opportunities. Meeting George (later Sir George) Gibb, general manager of the NER in the course of official business, Merz advised him to counter the electric tram threat to the NER Tyneside suburban network thus: 'Why don't you electrify your railway?' Gibb took the cue, and was probably thinking along those lines in any case. M & M produced a plan to electrify the Newcastle-

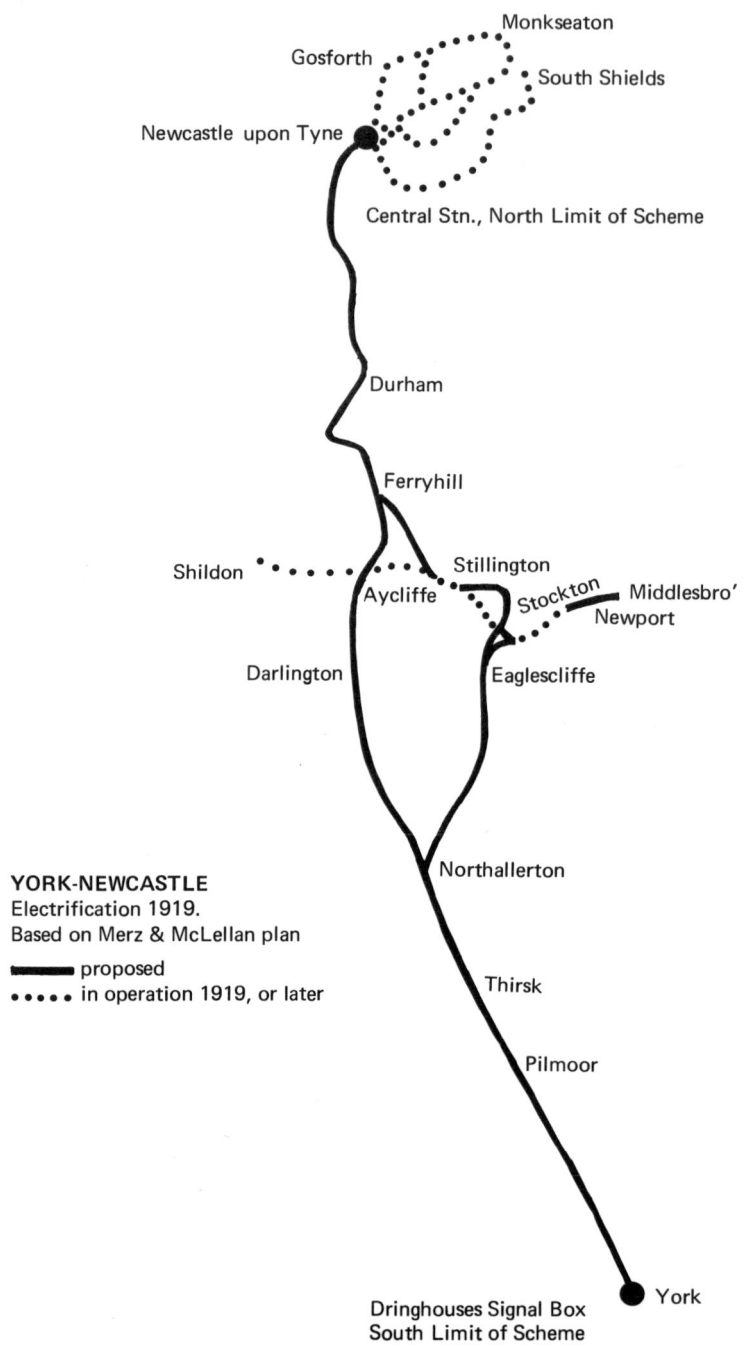

Monkseaton

Gosforth

South Shields

Newcastle upon Tyne

Central Stn., North Limit of Scheme

Durham

Ferryhill

Shildon

Stillington

Aycliffe

Stockton

Middlesbro'

Newport

Darlington

Eaglescliffe

YORK-NEWCASTLE
Electrification 1919.
Based on Merz & McLellan plan

Northallerton

━━━ proposed
•••• in operation 1919, or later

Thirsk

Pilmoor

York

Dringhouses Signal Box
South Limit of Scheme

Tynemouth line, and this bore fruit on 29th March 1904 when the first section, from New Bridge Street-Benton [2] was opened to electric traction. This was virtually the first electric suburban railway in Britain. [3] It was a resounding success, and more than restored lost traffic; after a drop of 4 million passengers per year between 1901-4 business picked up to 7.3 million (1908) and 10 million (1913). More important to our story, it had forged a close link between the NER and M & M. One aspect of M & M's advice that was adhered to in all NER electrification schemes was to buy power from extant power companies, in this case the Newcastle upon Tyne Electric Supply Company (NESCO) who built a further station at Carville to ease the growing demand caused by the coast line electrification. The railway used 600V d.c., transformed and fed into their network at twelve substations.

Simultaneously with the coast-line electrification, the NER converted the one-mile Quayside branch which ran down a long curve at 1 in 27/30 through a badly ventilated tunnel to the riverside railway network. Its topography was unideal for steam working, but perfect to show off the potential of two electric shunting locos [4] which played their part in propagating the new system of traction. All this success was further enhanced when M & M read a paper on the subject of Tyneside electrification to the meeting of the British Association at Cambridge in 1904.

It had been shown that electric traction could handle suburban commuter and tripper traffic, and had conquered the operating problem of the freakish [5] Quayside branch. The NER now turned to seeing if what the Americans call 'juice jacks' could help them with their staple traffic; i.e. shifting coal in bulk. The coal industry boomed, output was rising yearly to the 1913 all-time peak of 287 million tons. Against this background of successful electric traction and a guaranteed, rising demand for coal the NER decided to experiment with cost-cutting by electrifying the heavily used

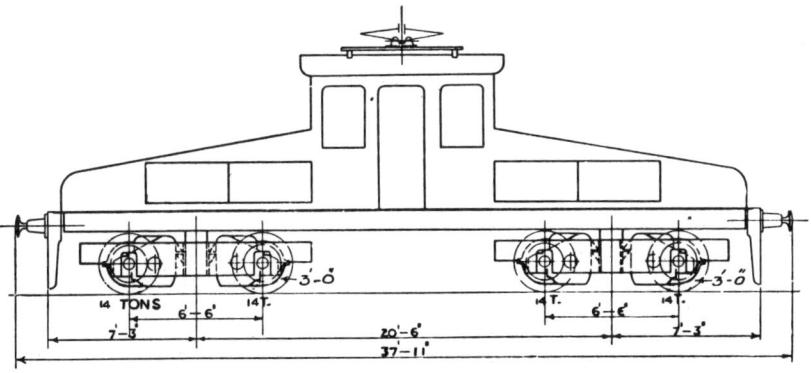

Bo-Bo Electric loco for Newcastle Quayside branch

Under the compound catenary: a Shildon-Newport coal train runs down to Teesside behind electric loco No. 11 (Bo-Bo). This engine was the longest lived of its class, its last duty being shunting at Ilford. It was withdrawn in 1964. *(British Rail)*

Shildon-Newport (S-N) line in County Durham. This took coal from near Bishop Auckland to Teesside, for the steel industry and for export. The well-tried connexion between the NER and M & M launched this new and successful venture. It was unusual for railway companies to employ consulting engineers; an unfortunate omission to judge by the excellent and imaginative results emanating from the Northumbrian partnership. Since 1904, M & M had enriched their experience of electric traction by advising on schemes in Australia, Argentina and India. All this was to help the 1913 Shildon-Newport scheme.

On the S-N line, the NER decided to employ electric locos which were to be much larger than the Quayside shunters. Power was purchased from the Cleveland & Durham Electric Power Company (closely associated with Charles Merz and NESCO), but in this case it was converted to 1,500V d.c. Also, whereas Tyneside used third-rail electrification (except in the Quayside line yards), S-N employed overhead copper wires as conductors. Shildon (Middridge Junction) to Newport (Erimus Yard) was 15 miles[6] and this basic spine fell 340 feet in 14¼ miles of its distance. Trains of up to 1,400 tons did the journey in just less than an hour. The line was opened to electric traction on 1st July 1915[7] but its career was overshadowed by the post-war decline of the coal trade. It was an operational success, but a financial failure. Dwindling traffic did not justify the heavy basic cost of electric traction, and the line reverted to steam haulage in January, 1935.

Such sad matters lay in the future when S-N was opened. Its success in the early days played a big part in the York-Newcastle (Y-N) electrification story. To both the Y-N scheme, and to general railway electrification, the S-N line was a source of much empirical data.[8] The ten S-N locos were one of the strongest influences on the Y-N electrification; their success convinced their designer Vincent (later Sir Vincent) Raven of the inherent superiority of electric traction. Raven, a personal friend of Merz, was a highly proficient steam-engine designer with a lucid and objective intellect. In 1913 an acolyte in matters electrical, by 1919 he had become a high-priest. As the NER's Chief Mechanical Engineer, the task of designing the engines fell to Raven. He had them built at the NER workshops at Darlington, the electrical equipment being supplied by Siemens. A diagram appears later (page 17); suffice it to say the locos were eminently satisfactory performers. All this impressed Raven the engineer. Unfortunately, whatever savings might be enjoyed by running electric as opposed to steam engines, there was no denying the heavy capital cost of electrification. It was this fact which was to decide the matter one way or the other when the moment of truth came.

Raven claimed, towards the end of the Y-N electrification plan's active life in 1922,[9] that in 1920 (which he called 'the last normal year' referring to the 1921 coal strike which cut into S-N traffic) that 5 electric locos did the work 'formerly done by 13 steam engines' on the S-N line. Costs ran at

Sir Vincent Raven, 1859-1934. *(British Rail)*

1½d per engine-mile whereas a steam engine needed 11½d per engine-mile. Referring to the rapid fall in prices of 1922, Raven went on to say, 'Present day cost, of course, is considerably below that of 1920'. Raven was cautious about running costs, but in an earlier paper [10] he admitted: 'The steam engine's coal and water and the equivalent electric engine's power cost about the same'. In his official report advocating the Y-N scheme (October 1919) Raven stated that total cost of working electric engines was 10.9d per train-mile, while steam cost 14.8d per train-mile.

The background to the Y-N scheme is now clear. The NER establishment, closely connected to Europe's leading electrical engineers, had tried electricity and found that it answered special operating problems. On broad, pragmatic grounds it was a success. Yet there were a few mines adrift unnoticed to the engineers and enthusiasts, and it was against these that the Y-N plan was to founder. There was a decline in the industrial structure of the North East. Prices were declining and interest rates fluctuated with unnerving instability, and this latter point was of great moment when the Board were faced with the need of finding large amounts of new capital. Hovering over the railway world was the Railways Act of 1921, which was to merge all railways into

Overhead maintenance train near Redmarshall South signal cabin on the Shildon line; what might have become a familiar sight between York and Newcastle. The gang is under chargehand N. Reule, and consists of Messrs. Wetherell, Eden, Foggin, Rolph, Richardson and the donor of this picture, J. A. Ainsley. Note J24 class loco, drum waggon and tower waggon converted from an old steam passenger coach.

four groups in 1923. All these matters were unsettling, and the high efficiency of the Shildon-Newport locos could not discount or obscure them.

It is doubtful whether anyone will ever know for certain in which mind the Y-N electrification plan was hatched. Clearly Raven was a great enthusiast of electrification by 1919, the year in which he returned to the NER after four years' work for the government. Merz wrote in his private notes that Francis Lydall (late of Siemens, then working for M & M, later a partner), he and Raven had many discussions in 1919 about pushing further electrification on the NER.[11] They plumped for the York-Newcastle main line, part of the King's Cross-Edinburgh trunk route, and by June 1919 M & M had produced a full feasibility study of the scheme. By October, Raven had added another, written jointly with the NER general superintendent, H. A. Watson. This was submitted to the NER Board. On the strength of these reports the board gave provisional approval late in 1919 to the Y-N scheme. This gave Raven sufficient encouragement to produce a main-line electric locomotive which was to be tested on the S-N line.

Unfortunately, by the time the engine was outshopped (May 1922) the whole Y-N scheme was clouded over. First, the scheme had been suspended pending a government investigation, and by the time this was over the railway

9

grouping was imminent. The NER was in its last throes as an independent entity: in 1923 it was merged into the London & North Eastern Railway which had to settle down before embarking on great schemes. Then it entered its long insolvency; it last paid a dividend on deferred ordinary stock in 1925! Delay and financial weakness scotched the plan conceived and launched by the single-minded enthusiasm of Merz and Raven. Nevertheless, the clear and vigorous reports of Raven and M & M give a full description of what might have been, and the high-speed electric locomotive, although late in appearance, was duly built at Darlington. From these ideas and artefacts we can piece together the story of what was very nearly Britain's first main-line electrification.

The Plan and its Fate

It was felt that the Shildon-Newport scheme, although successful, was not extensive enough to make a dent in the NER's operating expenses. On the other hand, the 80-mile stretch of main line from York to Newcastle carried one-eighth of the NER's total traffic. There was increasing pressure on the available track, and it seemed that either electrification, or quadrupling track, was necessary.

Quadrupling would be immensely expensive, electrification might well be cheaper and could cope with all types of traffic. The Y-N section was self-contained, i.e. it was logical to change locomotives anyway at major traffic nodes like Low Fell Yards or Newcastle Central Station, and the change could usefully be from steam to electricity or *vice versa,* making a virtue of necessity.

Because a large amount of goods traffic from York to Northallerton was *en route* to and from Teesside, it was also deemed logical to electrify from Northallerton to Newport Yard (via Eaglescliffe) and (with similar conditions holding North of Ferryhill) from Ferryhill to Middlesbrough via Stockton. The Y-N scheme would thus link up with the Shildon-Newport line (see map page 4) and at its northern extremity with the existing Tyneside electrification. [12] The *NER Magazine* of 1919 spoke of building an 'efficient network'. In private conversations Raven expanded sanguinely about electrifying to Carlisle and Berwick on Tweed.

M & M recommended that the 1,500V d.c. already employed on the Shildon line be further employed on Y-N; there were no tunnels so the overhead would be easy to erect. Here, however, we come to the major and perennial mystery of the Y-N scheme. M & M suggested third-rail conductor for current collection as a possibility, and this was warmly adopted by Raven, although he later cooled down and had apprently changed his mind by 1922. The original advocacy of third-rail was on grounds of cost. Raven estimated that third-rail would cost £2,850 per track-mile against overhead's £4,340.

10

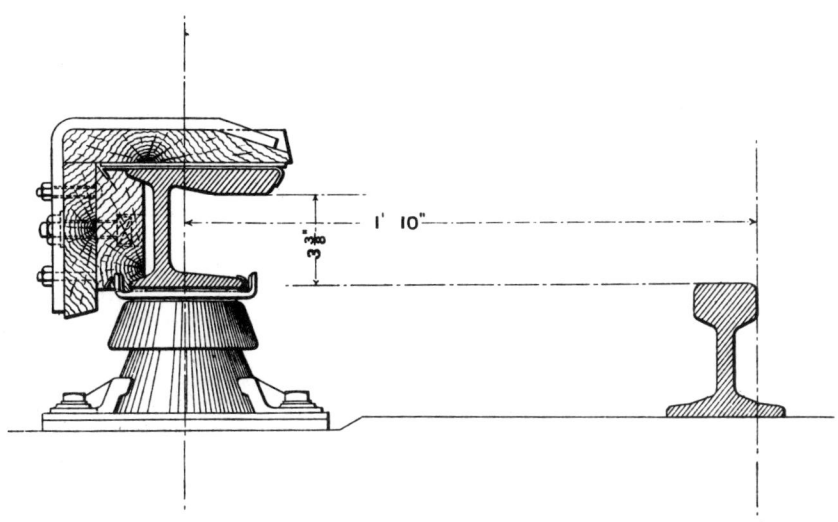

Wood protected under-contact third-rail for electric conductor as designed by
S. G. Redman of M & M for the Central Argentine Railway (electric service opened
1916) and suggested for use on the Y-N line. *(Merz & McLellan)*

Third-rail maintenance was more expensive than overhead, but its depreciation
less. There were good engineering reasons for third-rail also: it could be
maintained by the normal permanent way gangs; bridges and tunnels (in case
of extension) were no problem and it was 'a thoroughly sound mechanical
job' (M & M). The consulting engineers added that there were 'long stretches
of track between important towns without junctions or complications, and
where it is desired to run at high speed'.

Although third-rail was strongly advocated at first, even at that stage
there was seen to be a need for overhead work at big junctions or level
crossings in order to avoid 'gapping'. The overhead was to be erected at York,
Thirsk, Northallerton, Darlington, Ferryhill, Durham, Low Fell, Newcastle
Central and Stockton. There were to be 115 miles of overhead, 282 miles of
third-rail (in both cases track-miles, not route-miles). For safety's sake
M & M suggested the third-rail be partly boxed in wood, a precaution which
would marginally reduce the menace of frost and ice and the furious arcing
that these can cause. An example of the catenary gantries necessary at large
junctions, e.g. Thirsk, is given on page 12.

Still, third-rail for all its cheapness, had drawbacks. There was some
doubt as to whether an express engine could safely hit third-rail at (say)
70 mph with its bogie-mounted pickup shoes. Trials were arranged at
Strensall, near York, whereby a steam engine fitted with dummy pickup
shoes made contact with a third-rail at speed. The engine was an NER 4-4-4T
which had as close a structural layout to the putative electric locos as any
NER engine available. There were two further snags. In spite of the wooden

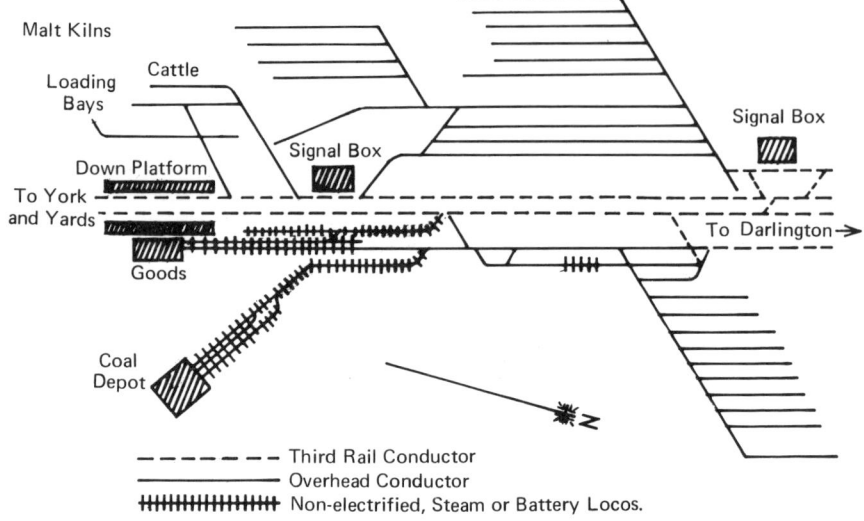

Malt Kilns

Loading Bays — Cattle

Down Platform

To York and Yards

Goods

Signal Box

Signal Box

To Darlington →

Coal Depot

N

– – – – – – – Third Rail Conductor
——————— Overhead Conductor
╫╫╫╫╫╫╫╫╫╫ Non-electrified, Steam or Battery Locos.

Diagram showing the proposed layout at Thirsk station (North end) under Raven's first plan

box, it was feared that 1,500V d.c. a few inches from platelayers' shins was asking for trouble. Above all there was the leakage problem; current (especially at high voltages) tends to leak to earth if near the ground and it was feared that the wastage would be high.[13] While Raven spoke confidently of third-rail in October 1919, by December 1921 he told J. Sayer in reply to a question arising out of a professional address that his intention was to collect current 'entirely from overhead and not to use third-rail'. So, in spite of first-cost advantages, Raven abandoned the third-rail scheme.[14]

Raven hoped to cover the Y-N tracks with electric power, leaving various goods yards and through roads (e.g. at Eaglescliffe) free of catenary (or third-rail under the original plan). Power would run for the first 100 yards into a marshalling yard, thereafter battery locos would take over. The NER would also electrify quarry and mine branches if the traffic source was less than two miles from the main line.

Electricity was to be purchased from existing power companies (M & M's well-tried advice) and in March 1921 the *Electrical Review* reported that negotiations to this end were taking place between the NER and NESCO. The Cleveland and Durham network had its equity capital bought by NESCO in 1917, so in effect the same firm supplied all power to the railway. M & M envisaged tapping the South Yorkshire Power Company's system if the electric line went on to Doncaster — one of the few official references to going beyond York or Newcastle. There were to be seven substations (York,

Pilmoor, Northallerton, Darlington, Ferryhill, Durham and Newcastle) each about 15 miles apart. The line was in fact deliberately 'over-substationed' to allow for an increase in future traffic. M & M calculated that the 1,500V d.c. would cost about ½d per unit 'at the third rail'; they and others drew attention to the relative cheapness of power in the North East, arising from the efficient organisation of NESCO and its (then) unusual regional network.

In a report of October 1919, Raven and H. A. Watson (General Superintendent, NER) dazzled the NER Board and senior officers with technology and comparative statistics. These tell us much of contemporary working and problems, and what sort of an electric line might have emerged; (the estimates assume use of the third-rail, however). It was claimed that the whole Y-N scheme would cost £1,302,800 for track equipment, plus £93,800 for signalling alterations. There would result a saving in working expenses of £121,025 p.a. [15] The new line would need 29 electric passenger locos at £12,800 each to replace 54 steam locos; also 80 electric freight engines at £11,500 each to replace 155 steam engines. Raven added that the NER steam stock was worn down by war service, and that the railway was 208 locos short of requirements, anyway. Although 109 electric locos would cost more than steam locos engine-for-engine, they could do the work of 209 steam engines; they hauled larger trains, and alterations at Low Fell, Ferryhill and Bradbury yards could enable the NER to run fewer, but bigger trains, thereby saving *inter alia* on crew wages. The 109 electric locos would save £186,468 p.a. in running costs. [16] Raven felt justified in deducting £440,200 from the total electrification cost on account of the greater effect of his 109 electric engines over the necessary (and notional) 209 steam engines. Taking this off £1,396,600 we have £956,400 as Raven's estimate of the Y-N scheme's cost. Obviously this was a broad guess, open to sniping by hawkish accountants and others, but it would be fair to say that the Y-N scheme was a 'million pound electrification'. This would be equivalent to about £4½ million at today's prices and one would certainly not get 100 or so miles of electrification for that in the 1970's! What a chance was lost, as Charles Merz later ruefully observed.

Having presented his June 1919 report, Merz went to South Africa for a while where he was responsible for the Union's railway electrification plans. Merz believed, in his later writings, that the Y-N scheme was 'in the bag' at the time of his going. Raven and Lydall went to the USA on a fact-finding tour. Their study of American electric railways confirmed their optimism.

While the engineers travelled and observed, politics began to shift at home. There was much ferment over the railway question. Should the muddled system of competing railways be nationalized or rationalized? The latter dogma won (Railways Act 1921) and was realized in the grouping of January, 1923. All this overshadowed the NER Board. Even before 1923 much preliminary co-ordination was taking place, and it is generally suspected that J. G. Robinson and H. N. (later Sir Nigel) Gresley, possible Chief Mechanical Engineers of the NER's successor (the London & North Eastern Railway) were unconvinced by Raven's enthusiastic claims. Gresley became CME of the LNER, and Raven was something of a 'lame duck' CME during his last months in harness, 1922-23. In any case the NER Board were unwilling to undertake large items of expenditure in this twilight organizational period.

However, with regard to electrification, there were additional complications. Other electrification schemes were also mooted at this time and there was concern over the possibility of a heterogeneous rash of systems being adopted. The recently-created Ministry of Transport could not afford a gaffe so early in its career, and requested the NER to put its plans on ice while an advisory committee deliberated the subject. This committee (chaired by Sir Alexander Kennedy) sat for a year (July 1920 – June 1921) in order to produce its findings. Merz, himself a member, regretted its tardiness and blamed this for the eventual demise of the Y-N plan. In so far as the climate for Raven's scheme was distinctly chilly by 1921, Merz was quite right. In fact the Kennedy Committee recommended the very items that M & M had already suggested to the NER: 3-phase a.c. distribution, 1,500V d.c. overhead or third-rail and various safety measures. The timing and results of this committee were cruelly ironical to Raven.

When the Kennedy Report eventually emerged, the economy was looking unhealthy, the brave days of 1919 seemed far away now, and it was not the 'glad confident morn' any more, especially in the North East. Nobody seriously disputed the *operating* advantage of electric traction, but at the same time nobody could overlook its high capital cost – especially as Raven had abandoned the cheaper third-rail system for overhead. The national pressure group for railway electrification (mainly a selection of railwaymen and electrical engineers) started to push the government (Conservative, Prime Minister Bonar Law) for state aid to electrify railways in general: [17] their schemes would have cost £50 million.

On 27th November 1922 the Cabinet Committee on Unemployment (by then about 14% and a source of great national anxiety) submitted its report to the full Cabinet. The Committee chaired by Sir Arthur Griffith-Boscawen, MP, Minister of Agriculture, had to say of electrification: We are glad to be able to report that the difficulties caused by the 'grouping' of the railway companies which have led to some delay in the progress of electrification . . . are being surmounted and that there is good reason to hope that these schemes involving £12 millions are likely to be commenced in . . . (the) near future'. Close on the heels of the Committee came a deputation of railway managers, led by Reginald McKenna[18] to press Bonar Law for financial help. The electrical press reported that the full cabinet discussed the matter on 30th November 1922, although Cabinet records show no evidence of this.

In any case, the government remained non-committal. It clearly hoped that the 1923 grouping would solve many of the railways' financial difficulties, or at least it used the grouping as an excuse for non-action. A year later nothing had been done by the government, and a group of 'industrial MP's' worried by the continuing high rate of unemployment and sluggish performance of the economy, openly demanded a massive programme of public works, including the Y-N scheme. The MP's spoke out in August 1923, when they noted interest rates were about 4%. They claimed that no railway scheme of electrification could offer more than a 4% rate of return, so a government guarantee was essential if capital was to be attracted. Still nothing happened: [19] the government had bigger problems, and public opinion was still suspicious of 'state interference' in the economy. By the time the NER was merged into the LNER the Y-N plan was as good as dead in any case. The LNER put a brave face on it, and even in the late 'twenties was dutifully reporting in the *Railway Year Book* that the Y-N scheme was still recognized. However, the LNER was impoverished; even if it had really wanted to carry out Raven's scheme (and there is no real evidence that it did) it lacked the necessary resources. [20]

The Y-N scheme was always backed more strongly by Raven than by the Board, which only gave provisional approval, and kept him short of funds (allowing but one engine, not the two he asked for). Delay confirmed their wisdom; by the time the engine was ready (May 1922) the NER was virtually at an end, the economy was depressed and Raven had switched to more expensive overhead current distribution. Many accounts claim that Y-N was killed by the LNER; the truth is that it was scotched before 1923. The North East, far from being the brightest jewel in the LNER crown, became a depressed liability. If the NER had survived it is highly unlikely Y-N would have gone ahead; if it had, then it would have been a costly burden to an unfortunate company serving the most depressed area of Great Britain. None of this, of course, detracts from its technical magnificence.

Following the Weir Report (1929) on railway electrification, M & M prepared a report for the LNER. This time the scheme was to run from London to Leeds and on to Nottingham, Lincoln and Grimsby. The North East did not even rate a mention: the 'affluent South' had arrived. In later years British Railways has undertaken considerable electrification, but its basic 1955 plan (as far as the North East is concerned) had a line from King's Cross to York. In any case, this was not built.

Back in the North East, the Shildon line reverted to steam traction in 1935 (and much of it was subsequently closed) and the historic Tyneside electric lines turned to diesel traction by 1967; the whole of the fine achievements of Raven and Merz became strictly historical. What a tale of gloom to compare with the euphoric days of 1919 when the Y-N was confidently expected to materialise; or when in February 1921 the

Newcastle Daily Chronicle said that the Newcastle-Darlington section of the scheme was about to start *en route* for York, and described it as 'one of the several schemes' of improvement. However, it would not be true to say that all this was in vain. Much was learned, and a great engine, No. 13 was built.

Locomotives

The Y-N scheme had a variety of proposed locomotives, and one was actually made. Raven's papers on this aspect of the subject, naturally his *forte*, are masterpieces of distilled information and argument on contemporary design. He generally delivered a broadside on the general advantages of electrification (enumerated in up to ten points) and then discussed the relative merits of the three main types of electric engine: rod-drive, gearless and quill-drive. His views reflected those of the M & M 1919 report. He favoured the latter two designs, fearing the vibration and maintenance problems on rod-drive locos. He chose a quill-drive (see page 29) passenger design and implied that a modified Shildon-type loco design would handle freight. For shunting there would be battery engines, or modified 'Quayside' types. The designs actual and proposed were as follows:

Worm-drive O-C-O (or 1-A-1)
Raven converted a steam-engine tender to have vertical worm-drive on the middle axle. The motor was carried on the tender frame in an attempt to see if the axle deadweight could be reduced. This 31-ton 8 cwt loco was an experiment; however, it was fitted with pick-up shoes, given a makeshift cab, and tried between Jesmond and Gosforth on the Tyneside coast lines. It was not a success, and has always remained something of an enigma.

Notional Co + Co
In his Paris paper, Raven illustrated an articulated box-cab freight loco, with quill-drive. It was to be 'capable of a pull of 15 tons which would haul a train of 1,000 tons up a gradient of 1 in 100 at 30 mph . . . something we ought to aim at in the future.' Whether he intended to employ this 108-ton giant is not known. He set it up besides an equally hypothetical 134-ton 0-8-2 steam engine, its theoretical twin in strength.

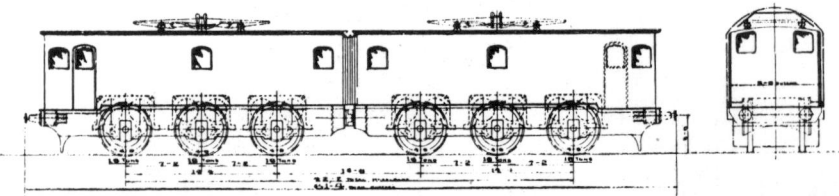

Proposed Co+Co articulated loco

16

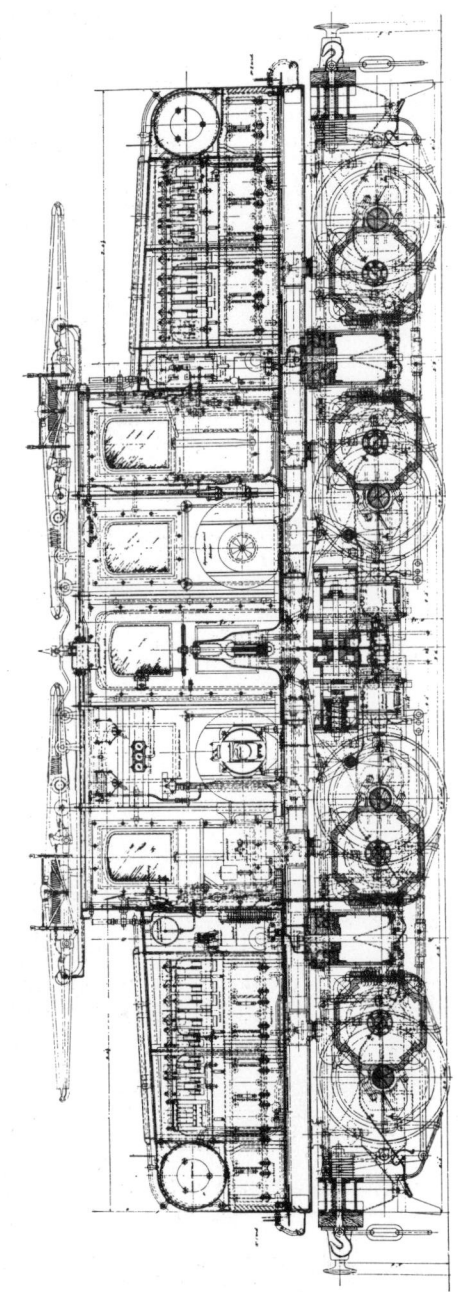

Plan of a Shildon-Newport electric loco

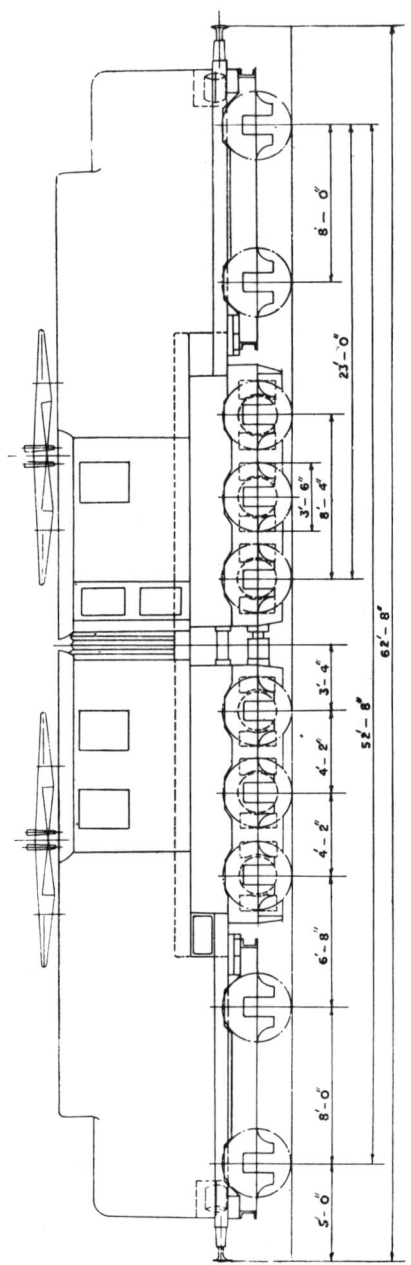

Proposed gearless loco (2-Co+Co-2) as suggested by GEC

Modified Shildon-Newport Bo-Bo

This was for freight and mineral traffic. The modification (suggested by M & M) was in the motors, but no details were forthcoming.

Gearless articulated 2-Co + Co-2

This was actually designed by the General Electric Company of America at their Schenectady works, following Raven's visit when he was on tour with Francis Lydall. It was designed to the same specifications that produced No. 13 (see page 27), but was entirely different in form. It was to have been 62' 8" long, to weight about 105 tons and have six 300-hp motors. It was a close relative in design to some GEC locos built for the Milwaukee Road.[21] Raven could not persuade the NER board to build the engine, though he tried. One wonders about its suitability at 90 mph, the maximum required of it.

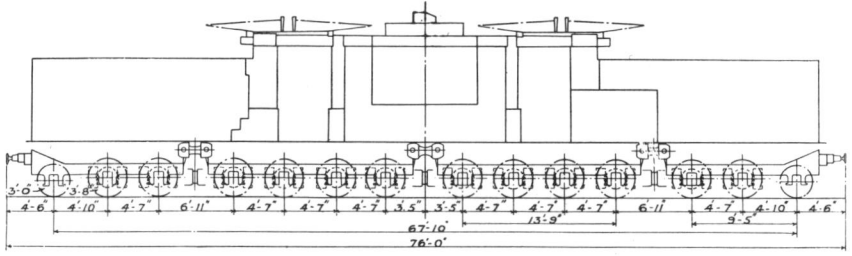

Milwaukee Road 4,020 h.p. gearless loco (1-Bo-Do+Do-Bo-1) which inspired the figure on page 18

Merz & McLellan designs, submitted in June 1919

There was a gearless and a geared-quill design for ordinary passenger and heavy passenger work. Of the four designs, this is particularly interesting, being the inspiration almost to the detail of No. 13. M & M thought the light passenger loco sufficient for most Y-N needs; the three driving axle version was an 'extra powerful' type for arduous duty. By choosing it, Raven played safe; it could shift any conceivable passenger load in Northumbria. It followed the GEC-Milwaukee Road quill-drive designs quite closely, with certain important modifications made to increase availability, e.g. slotted quills for easier axle inspection.

No. 13: a quill-drive 2-Co-2

This was built at Darlington NER workshops. This engine operated on tests for a few months in late 1922, before entering a long hibernation in storage, and eventual scrapping (1950). Technical data, etc. are given in the Appendix, but there are several important background facts regarding the engine. Before she emerged from the workshops in May 1922 she had been assembled by the company's own staff, although all electrical equipment was made by Metropolitan-Vickers at their Trafford Park, Manchester works.

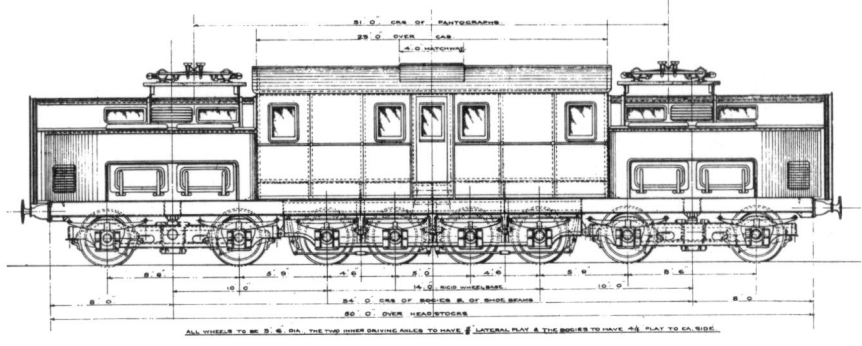

(a)

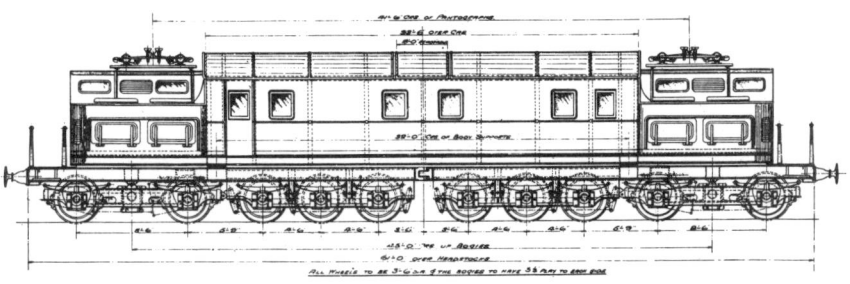

(b)

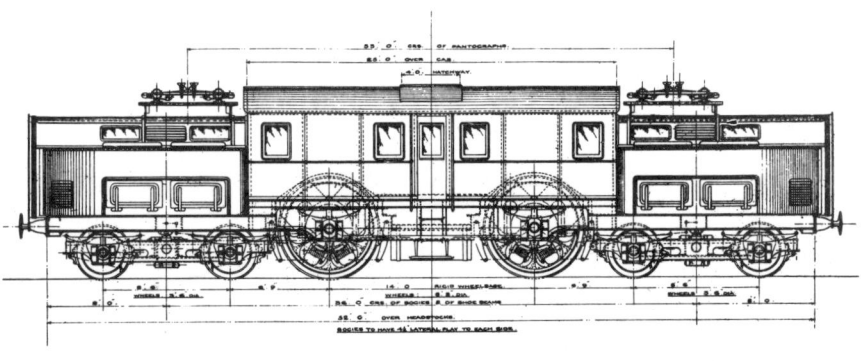

(c)

M & M suggested designs of 1919: *(a)* light gearless; *(b)* heavy gearless; *(c)* light quill-drive; *(d) facing page:* heavy quill-drive—the progenitor of No. 13. *(Merz & McLellan)*

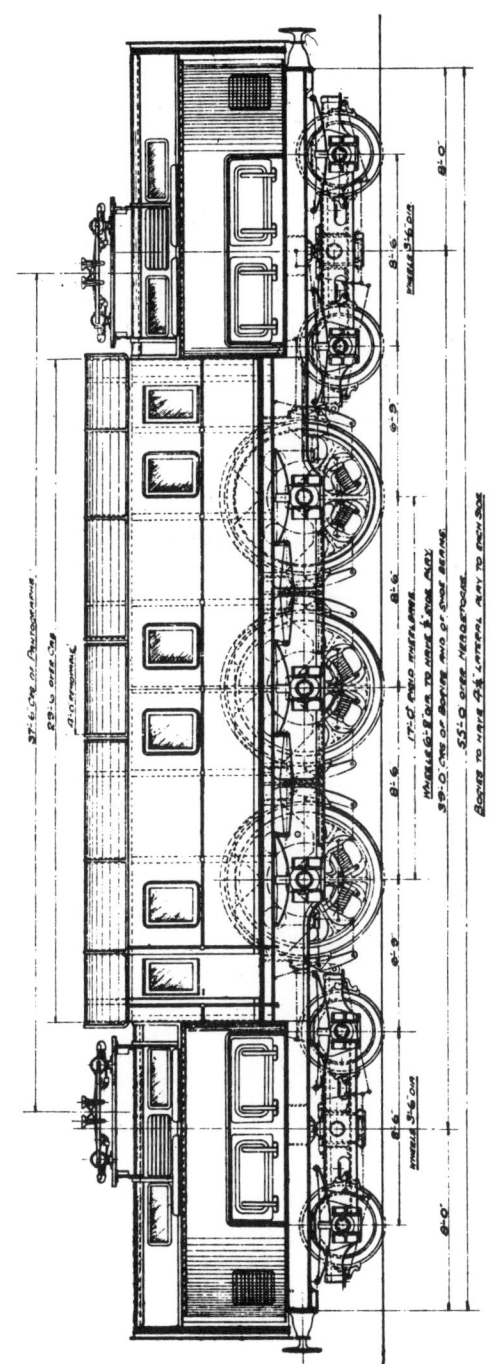

(d)

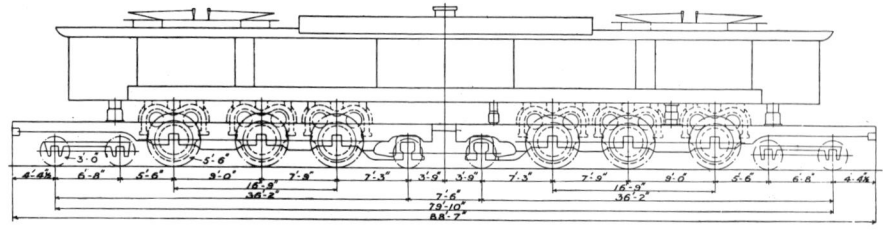

Milwaukee Road 4,680 h.p. quill-drive design (2-Co-1+1-Co-2) showing similar layout of motors as in No. 13 (below)

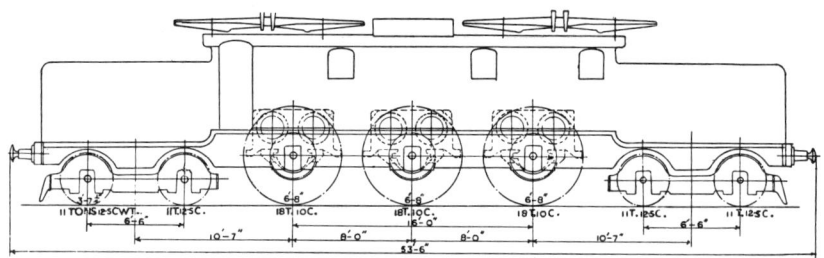

The NER staff incorporated this into the 'mechanical and engineering' frame which was theirs entirely. Metrovick had a representative at Darlington (R. T. Brookes) as liaison officer. By a happy coincidence, M & M's man on the spot was Norman Raven, the CME's son. No. 13's design was really 'modified M & M' with strong transatlantic influences. It must be remembered, however, that Raven was involved in many of the Merz-Lydall conversations of Spring 1919, and was a fine engineer in his own right. The design may not have been his completely, but he was certainly no 'front man'.

No. 13's most striking feature was the set of six immense driving wheels (6' 8") with their six half-spokes and six sets of trifurcated spokes,[22] so designed to resist the massive pressures of the quill drive. Their effect was aesthetic, although their motive was purely functional. Those who remember No. 13 operating under power still wax enthusiastic on the subject. On starting, the giant helical springs which pressed on the spokes would suddenly compress. Then she would move away with startling acceleration: thrilling, occult and swift. All this was especially impressive to observers accustomed to the noisy pyrotechnics of the steam locomotive. B. K. Cooper once wrote of No. 13's impact: 'a handsome design made familiar in the railway books and on the cigarette cards of its day, yet with something of the remoteness of a space ship.' F. J. G. Haut described it in his monumental work *The History of the Electric Locomotive* as 'years ahead of its time'. Aesthetically, No. 13 was perhaps the finest electric engine ever built, with her enormous driving wheels (the largest ever on an electric engine), geometric sandboxes and lined green finish. Like most electric and diesel engines she was a mechanical

No. 13 in pristine condition, with pantographs down. *(EE-AEI Traction)*

No. 13 at Bowesfield, Autumn 1922. Driver (in forward cab) William Hopper; charge fitter (rear cab) Robert Brownless; on *terra firma,* Ralph Robson, Chief Draughtsman at Darlington. *(R. Brownless)*

palindrome, in obvious contrast to the uni-directional steam loco. However, the placing of one cab door per side, and the general use of a single pantograph gave her the slight and necessary asymmetry associated with moving vehicles. There was a certain abruptness about the three-quarter view, but nothing that imaginative lining-out could not have cured.

Through the summer and autumn of 1922, No. 13 was put through her paces on the Shildon line, often with the NER dynamometer car attached in order to gather technical data about her behaviour. The railwaymen at Shildon sheds were a ready-made team of electrical experts, including the shedmaster, J. W. Thackeray, the charge fitter, R. Brownless, and a number of drivers used to electric engines, notably William Hopper, who tended to become No. 13's principal operator. Casting an experienced eye over No. 13, Brownless thought the contactors rather too small, and had sufficient faith in his hunch to order a light engine to stand by in case of trouble on the first test.

Sure enough, when approaching Bowesfield with no fewer than 22 carriages[23] on this test, No. 13 burnt out at the contractors and came to a halt. Sir Vincent's 'Special' drew up, and the CME bore down on the assembled gathering about the still engine. Brownless caught him and explained the trouble; Sir Vincent had got into something of a state by this time, and hectored the assembled party of pundits. He spun on his heels, and barked to his personal driver: 'To Darlington', abandoning many of his own party, and leaving the experts looking po-faced beside the mute No. 13. Brownless suggested to R. T. Brookes (the Metrovick man) that he had better get to Darlington before the 'old man' and head off his wrath. Brookes hired a taxi, only to find a message awaiting him at North Road Works 'Phone Sir Vincent at his private house at once.' This he did, receiving an order from the still-simmering chief to get No. 13 operational within the week. Trafford Park worked against the clock and sent up the replacements by car within seven days: much might depend on the outcome of No. 13's tests.

After this high drama, the rest of No. 13's life was something of a decline. She made more test trips, and at least two journeys to Erimus yard with a full load. Once she hauled a train of empties back to Shildon, together with the failed electric loco which occasioned this unique performance. William Hopper drove her for visiting parties of directors and 'railway brass', and other drivers took turns to get the feel of manoeuvering her. Then all was silence — or nearly so. She reapperared on July 25th, 1925 for the railway centenary celebrations at Darlington, somewhat ignominiously hauled by a small tank engine (LNER No. 1163). For long years she rested in the paint shop at Darlington, joined in 1935 by her Shildon cousins; in 1946 the LNER renumbered her No. 6999. There was talk of using her on the Manchester-Wath electrification, but nothing came of it. In 1947 she was moved to Gosforth car sheds (her only trip ever from Darlington to Newcastle) and three years later (as BR No. 26600) she was officially withdrawn. On 15th December 1950 she was hauled behind a K1 class steam engine (No. 62058) to Messrs. Wanty of Catcliffe near Rotherham where she was scrapped — the last vestige of a great idea.

Really the Y-N plan died with the NER in December 1922, although it was moribund for a year before that. No. 13 was a ghostly reminder of bolder times. What the world lost! An apple green 'Baltic electric' with varnished teak coaches shimmering through the Vale of York of a summer evening, or picking herself adroitly over Newcastle Central's 'biggest diamond crossing in the world'. Another North-Easterner, Lord Eustace Percy [24] called the inter-war

No. 13 on test with a 17-coach train, including dynamometer car (in front): a glimpse of what might have been.

establishment 'men of little spirit'. Perhaps, to them the strategy of Raven and Merz was a cyclopean project inherited from another age, and they could not rise to it. Could we?

Myth and Fact

In the years following the death of the Y-N plan there has been a luxuriant growth of railway literature and lore. References to the scheme have often perpetuated understandable but erroneous legends. First that the LNER killed the scheme. It did not, the NER had lost interest before 1923, although Raven remained as keen as ever. If there is any one 'villain' it is the year's delay of the Kennedy Committee which made its report just as the depression hit the North East. Secondly, that Raven designed No. 13 – in fact it was based on M & M designs which in turn were American-influenced. Raven, Merz and Lydall take joint credit for its design, and Raven (as CME) sole responsibility. Finally that Raven, a steam engineer, gave No. 13 large driving wheels because steam express engines had wheels of large diameter. It is true that fast steam engines do have such wheels, but for entirely different reasons. The advantages suggested by M & M for an electric engine with large drivers were: (i) higher centre of gravity therefore kinder to the track at high speeds, and (ii) ability to get frame-mounted motors which in turn are part of the sprung weight of the engine. An incidental advantage was that the frame-mounted motors were far more accessible than axle-mounted ones. It should be remembered that No. 13 was the product of world leaders in the field of electrical and mechanical engineering.

ACKNOWLEDGEMENTS

Above all I must thank Messrs Merz & McLellan for letting me look through and use old records; also British Railways for the same. Mr R. Brownless, sometime shed superintendent at South Gosforth, gave freely of his long and accurate memory. Other ex-railwaymen who have helped me are Mr J. A. Ainsley and Mr J. T. Forster, and I must also thank Mrs William Hopper. The *Northern Echo* put me in touch with these people. The North East Coast Institution of Engineers and Shipbuilders let me consult their records. The Cabinet Office, the Ministry of Transport and the Keeper of Public Records gave prompt help; English-Electric AEI Traction Ltd. let me have the photo on page 23 and some useful data; my colleague Mr L. Meaken gave unsparingly of his encyclopaedic railway knowledge and his very limited spare time, to help with the spadework.

APPENDIX

Technical data relating to No. 13
Dimensions

Length over buffers	53' 6"
Width overall	8' 10"
Total wheelbase	43' 8"
Fixed wheelbase	16' 0"
Driving wheel diameter	6' 8"
Bogie wheel diameter	3' 7¼"
Weight	102 tons (one source: 110 tons 1 cwt.)
Height (pantograph down)	13' 0⅛"
Weight per driving axle	18 tons 10 cwt
Weight per bogie axle	11 tons 12½ cwt
Tractive effort	15,900 lbs (1 hour) 9,480 lbs (continuous)
Speed	at 43 mph at 51½ mph
Horse power	1,800
Centre of gravity	4' 10" above rail level

Operational. Specifications demanded that she should start a 458-ton train on a 1 in 78 gradient without strain, and could also shift a 14-coach main-line train (450 tons) at 65 mph, and rise to 90 mph is necessary. It must be noted that the 90 mph was for emergencies; she was not expected to travel at that speed as a matter of course. It is doubtful whether timetables or track could have stood it for long! Estimates as to her highest speed vary widely. The unofficial estimates of observers are between 60 and 85 mph. If an average is any guide it would seem to be about 65 mph. The Shildon line was not designed for such treatment, although it stood up to it well. On test, No. 13 exerted a tractive effort of 8-10,000 lbs at 30 mph. Raven thought she could manage a 600-ton goods train with ease, all to the best: 'a reasonable load for a return trip of a passenger engine'— perhaps No. 13 might be classed a mixed traffic engine if this became common practice.

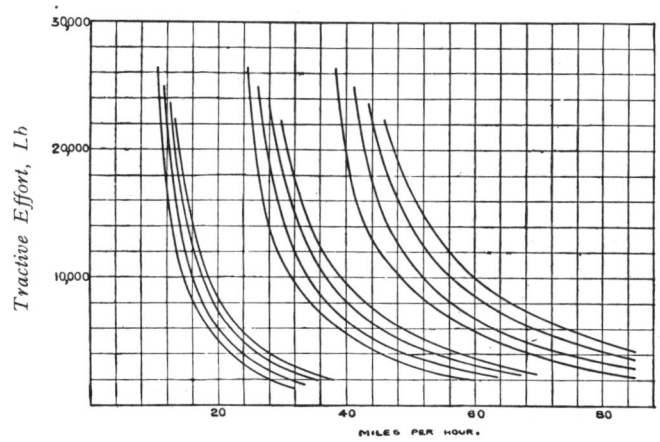

Tractive effort and speed curves of No. 13

27

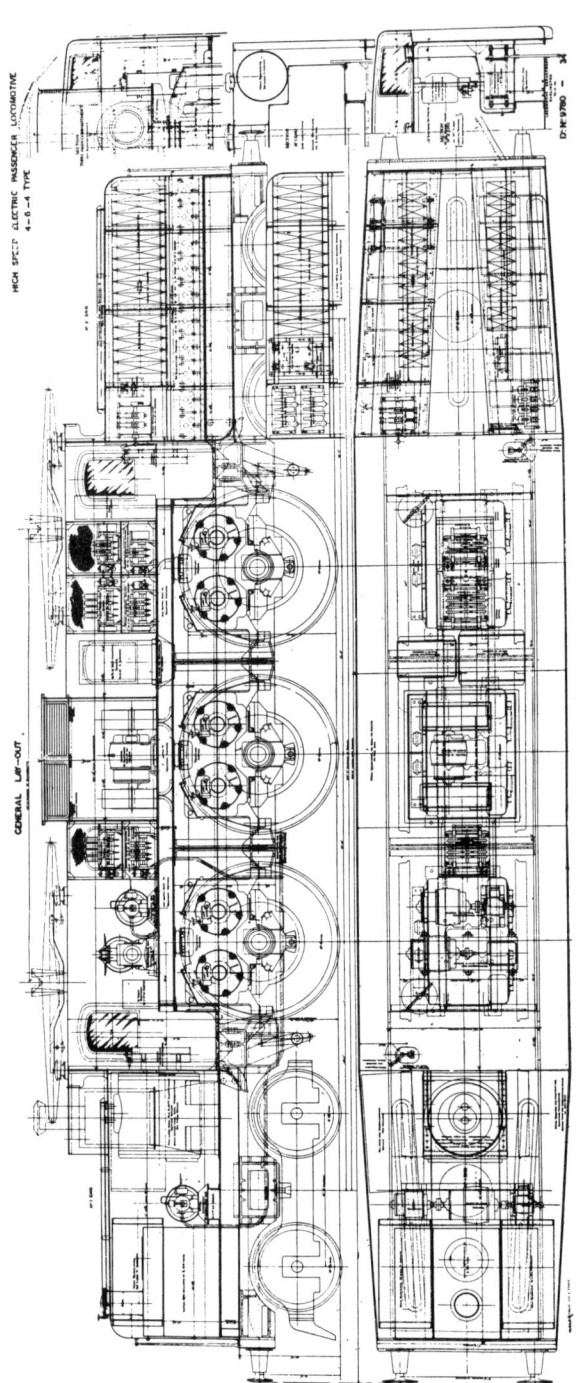

No. 13, general layout

M & M thought the severest natural test in traffic for an electric loco on Y-N was starting a 420-ton train up the 1 in 120 out of Durham. No 13 could take a 450-ton passenger train at 65 mph on the level 'under any ordinary conditions of weather', the t/e at 65 mph being 8,400 lbs (3¾ tons).

Motors and Drive. The quill-drive alluded to (p. 16) was an early attempt to get flexible drive and mount motors on the main frame, not the bogie or axles. Raven described it thus: 'Concentric with (the) axle a hollow shaft or quill, carrying at each end a spider (the arms of which) mesh with the spokes of the driving wheels . . . connected to them by springs. The quill carries a gear wheel which engages with the gear wheels of the pair of motors. The quill runs in 'suspension' bearings which form part of the motor frame, and the distance between the gear centres is thus definitely maintained.' The controls were electro-pneumatic and could select the six 300 hp motors as follows: (i) in series; (ii) as three sets of 2 in parallel; (iii) as two sets of 3 in parallel. Each combination permitted full field, or reductions of 18%, 31%, or 40%—thus there were twelve working speeds in all.

Boiler. Passenger comfort in northern winters was maintained by an electric boiler of 144 fire tubes containing quartz elements excited at 1,500 V d.c., and this could generate 1,000 lbs of steam at 120 lbs/sq. in. per hour.

Miscellaneous. No. 13 was dual-fitted (air and vacuum brakes) to work all types of stock. She had two independent air whistles and could give a chime or a shriek. She was very quiet when running, and had no gear whine, the gears being hand-honed for full and perfect contact. General opinion is that she never exceeded 65 mph (see above) but at that speed ran as steady as a rock. Raven corresponded with some CME's who had experience of running 4-6-4 tank engines by way of gathering empirical data about this nicely balanced wheel arrangement. She had right-hand drive, with a small driver's seat. Layout was such that one bonnet housed the boiler, the other the high-tension apparatus. The main compartment (27' long) was like a long room, housing the auxiliary machinery, also an electric ring to 'brew up' as befits the first English electric locomotive for a main line.

Models of No. 13 are to be found (there is one in the Science Museum, London) and there are illustrations in many of the works listed in the Bibliography (p. 32).

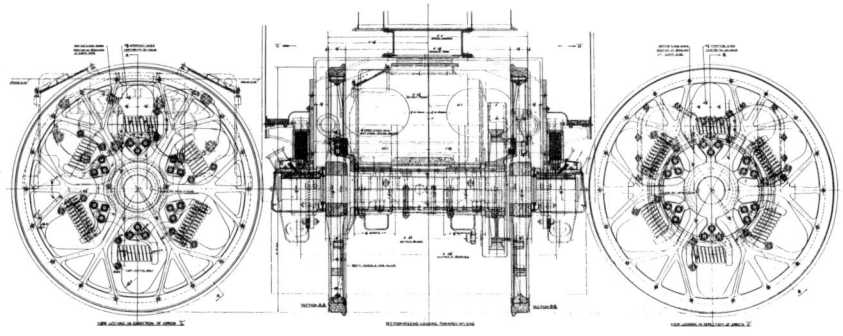

Quill drive assembly

29

Telegrams:
"Metrovick, Manchester."
Telephone 190/7 Trafford Park.

ADVICE NOTE.

METROPOLITAN-VICKERS ELECTRICAL CO., LTD.,

TRAFFORD PARK,
MANCHESTER.

To Messrs.

192

...rth Eastern Railway Co,

Chief Mechanical Engineer's
Office
Darlington

MARK.	Darlington

Dear Sirs,

28.6.22

We advise the despatch of the undermentioned Goods
consigned in accordance with your instructions.

Advice Note No.	G. 40131
Your Order	
Our Order	B64320.
Per	L&Y&NE Rly.
Carriage	Paid
Date Despatched	922

Box No.	Quantity	DESCRIPTION OF APPARATUS
		Shipping Address: North Eastern Railway, North Road Locomotive Works, Darlington,
	2	Cab' Heaters Dwg A 461134. SO"B" FR"C" 87585 (ETN) (H Traction)
		Partial S'ment
		Newcastle Traction.

In accordance with Railway Co.'s Bye-law it is necessary to advise us of non-delivery of goods within
14 days hereof, otherwise no claim can be established for total loss.

PACKING CASES value £ : will be charged for if not returned to above address CARRIAGE PAID, within one month.

GOODS DAMAGED OR INJURED IN TRANSIT.—All goods should be signed for "Received Unexamined." If goods are
found to have been damaged a claim against carrier must be made by the purchaser within three days of receiving goods.
The Metropolitan-Vickers Electrical Co. Ltd. will not be responsible for damage or loss in transit.

Advice note for parts sent up from Metrovick to Darlington, North Road
works. Note official code 'Newcastle Traction'

NOTES

(1)   The two rival companies, the Newcastle Upon Tyne Electric Supply Company (Pandon Dene Power Station) and the Newcastle & District Electric Lighting Company (Forth Banks Power Station) carved up the city by an agreement which they honoured until nationalization in 1948.

(2)   The rest of the coast lines system was electrified by June 1904, as was the Riverside loop. Newcastle-South Shields was electrified much later, in 1938.

(3)   Some London tube railways had already been electrified, and the Lancashire & Yorkshire Railway's Liverpool-Southport electric service started one week before, 22nd March 1904.

(4)   These were double bogie (Bo-Bo) centre-cab loco's, weighing 55 tons apiece, powered by four 160-hp motors which enabled them to haul 335 tons on the level at 14 mph, or 166 tons up the gradient at 9½ mph.

(5)   Its tunnel was a hairpin shape, hence both ends faced west and it could not ventilate in certain wind conditions.

(6)   Although F. A. W. Mann, *op. cit.*, says that by 1923 the S-N system totalled 18½ route-miles and 50 single track-miles.

(7)   Middridge Sidings-Bowesfield, 1/7/15; Shildon-Middridge Sdgs, 30/10/15; Bowesfield-Erimus, 12/11/15; and Erimus-Newport East, 1/1/16.

(8)   For example, the overhead gantries supporting the wires were placed at 300' intervals, but the winds of the County Durham uplands whipped the wires off loco pantographs. Intermediate gantries were put in, and the British standard has always been thereafter 210' to 220'. The contact wires (double for good contact) were hung from a main and an auxiliary wire (= 'compound catenary'). This suspension system, with single contact wires, became popular. The C & DEP Co. supplied 20k V a.c. to a substation at Aycliffe, and 11k V a.c. to another at Erimus.

(9)   The Paris address, 1922, see Bibliography, p. 32.

(10)   NECIE & S, 1921, see Bibliography, p. 32.

(11)   Raven's first publicized 'kite flying' on the Y-N scheme was in the *Proceedings of the Institute of Electrical Engineers*, February 1919, when he praised the reliability of electric traction and drew attention to the congestion between York and Newcastle, which could only be solved by quadrupling the track, or by electrification.

(12)   But note: Tyneside was electrified at 600V d.c.; the Y-N (proposed) at 1,500V d.c. Raven made no mention of a deliberate link at Newcastle; indeed he stated the extremities of the scheme to be Dringhouses signal-box at York, and Newcastle Central Station.

(13)   A warning of what might happen was in the 1915 electrification of 93 miles of the Michigan Railway, USA. Here there was third-rail electrification at 2,400V d.c., this resulted in severe arcing, burn-outs and passengers being herded into 'loading pens' to keep them away from the terrible menace of the 'hot rail'. The scheme was later modified to 1,200V d.c.: one winter proved enough!

(14)   It has been claimed that No. 13 had pickup shoes and bogie mounted shoebeams when stationed at Shildon in 1922, but I have been unable to verify this.

(15)   Savings estimated: wages, £53,197; coal, £110,122; stores, £10,395; repairs, £107,931; depreciation, £4,873. Total savings: £186,468 *less* new maintenance £65,443. Total net savings £121,025 p.a.

(16)   Running costs (p.a.): steam, £658,865; electric, £472,397. Electric locos would depreciate at £14,294 the lot, steam at £19,167 (assuming depreciation at %5 p.a.).

(17)   In addition to Y-N, parts of the SE & CR and LB & SCR (these were later carried out by the Southern Railway); parts of the Midland Railway, and of the GWR, especially the East and West valleys of Monmouthshire.

(18)   Chairman of the Midland Bank, sometime Chancellor of the Exchequer.
(19)   Although Colonel O'Brien, chief electrical engineer of the LMS, delivered a famous paper to the Institution of Electrical Engineers in 1924 in which he claimed '5 to 10% returns' on capital invested in electrification. This was highly optimistic: significantly, O'Brien was edged out of the LMS by the jungle politics which characterized that line in its early years.
(20)   Its early official schemes were well away from York: King's Cross-Hatfield (1923) and Liverpool Street-Gidea Park (1928). In later years the LNER did electrify the latter, also the Manchester-Sheffield main line. Another lingering gesture deferring to Y-N was the small vignette of No. 13 on public timetables even in the late 'twenties, by which time the credibility gap of the Y-N plan was fairly wide.
(21)   The Chicago, Milwaukee, St. Paul & Pacific RR, which had completed America's first really long-distance electrification of some 660 miles across the Rocky and Bitter Root Mountains, 1915-1920. Being the latest thing, it was closely studied. One of its huge gearless engines which inspired the GEC design for Raven is to be found in the St. Louis Museum of Transportation.
(22)   At the risk of undue pedantry it ought to be pointed out that the main spokes continued to the rim; the half spokes were of slightly different design.
(23)   Of the East Coast Joint Stock, i.e. jointly owned by the East Coast railway companies.
(24)   Sometime President of the Board of Education, and Minister without Portfolio, between the wars.

BIBLIOGRAPHY

R. Bell, *Twenty Five Years of the North Eastern Railway 1898-1922.*
Electric Railway Society Journal, especially March-April 1959.
Electrical Review, passim 1919-1923, especially December 1921 and January 1922 (Raven's papers).
F. J. G. Haut, *The History of the Electric Locomotive.*
K. Hoole, *The North Eastern Electrics.*
Proceedings of the Institution of Electrical Engineers, February 1919.
Merz & McLellan, *Memorandum: North Eastern Railway—Extension of Electrification* (confidential, June 1919).
North Eastern Railway Magazine, especially 1913 and 1920.
Railway Engineer, February, August and July 1922.
Railway Magazine, especially B. K. Cooper, 'Electrification Enters the Scene' (July 1957); K. Hoole, 'Electric Locomotives of the NER' (December 1959); F. A. W. Mann, 'Early Electrification in North East England' (May 1967).
Sir Vincent Raven, 'Railway Electrification', a paper read to the North East Coast Insittution of Engineers and Shipbuilders 16 December 1921. 'Electric Locomotives', a paper read to the Instituion of Mechanical Engineers at Paris, June 1922. (with H. A. Watson) Report on electrification to the NER Board, October 1919, *Railway Electrification in the USA.*
John Rowland, *Progress in Power* (private book written for M & M).

Film: *Darlington Centenary,* (British Transport Films) discovered in a cellar under the old Great Central Hotel and containing a picture of No. 13 being hauled along for viewing by the Duke of York, later King George VI.